I0059518

Shortcut Secrets to Creating High Profit Products

By T.J. Rohleder

Copyright © MMIX Direct-Response Network. All Rights Reserved.

Also by T.J. Rohleder:

Table of Contents

Introduction

Hello there! I'm T.J. Rohleder, co-founder of M.O.R.E., Inc. in Goessel, Kansas, and I want to thank you for investing in this shortcut system for creating a high profit book or manual that you can sell by mail or on the Internet. I think you'll find that this is an exciting publication. In these pages, I'll describe dozens of powerful and proven ways that you can make huge profits with your own books, manuals, or other informational products. **You're going to discover how it's possible to earn massive profits of up to $100,000 a year or more, with informational products that you can quickly and easily produce.** Best of all, you can make money with these products year after year -- and it's much easier than you ever imagined.

This publication is based on an audio product of the same name which I produced in association with six of my friends and colleagues: Alan R. Bechtold of BBS Press Service in Topeka, Kansas; Don Bice of the Direct Marketing Training Center in Glendale, California; Jeff Gardner of Success Achievement in Carlsbad, New Mexico; Russ von Hoelscher of Publisher's Media and the Hoelscher Marketing Group of El Cajon, California; Chris Lakey of Midwest Publishing in Newton, Kansas; and Mark Nolan, publisher of the Mark Nolan Letter in Sacramento, California. As for me, I'm the marketing director for M.O.R.E., Inc.

All seven of us are experts in creating best-selling informational products in very short periods of time, and as such, we've all learned some fabulous, effective shortcut strategies that we've used to bring in literally tens of millions of dollars. In this book, **I'll be sharing those same secrets with you.** I'll teach you how to create valuable products that people want and for which they are willing to pay big bucks, both in hardcopy and on the Internet. Even if you don't consider yourself a writer, you'll learn ways to make the writing process as quick and simple, so you can wring the most profit out of it in the shortest amount of time.

I look at writing as a recipe. To succeed in this business, I think it's very important that you consider yourself as a teacher, and learn to think in a step-by-step process that you can easily pass on to your readers. **When you approach your subject in this way, you're telling your reader exactly what they need to do each step of the way -- so the teaching becomes the focus, not the writing.** Which means you're not interested in your literary skills as much as your communication skills.

Thinking in terms of teaching rather than writing can be extremely effective. You just have to learn to conduct simple conversations on paper. If you can explain to someone sitting across the table from you how to accomplish something that they want to accomplish, then you can write and create top-quality, hot-selling products.

Many of us in the field -- including Russ von Hoelscher, who's been in self-publishing for almost forty years -- started as spare-time writers. Russ, for example, was always fascinated by writing, and had the good fortune of having a girlfriend in high school who was very intellectual and got him into reading all sorts unusual literature, including the French existentialists like John Paul Sartre. **He grew fascinated with books, especially fiction -- though now, of course, the only thing he's involved with is non-fiction moneymaking books and similar publications.** Back then, in the 1960s, he became so interested in science fiction that he started to submit stories to science fiction magazines -- and after a few tries, a pulp magazine accepted one of his stories, "The Women of Amazonia." He got $60 for 4,500 words. Later, of course, he became involved with self-publishing projects and mail order, **which was where the real money was**, and he never looked back.

While it's never too late to get into the lucrative self-publishing industry, I want you to know that it's never too early, either. I know two bright young men who started out, literally, as teenagers.

Jeff Gardner began his first mail order business when he was sixteen, at a time when most guys are seriously getting into high school sports and wondering who they'll ask to the prom.

Chris Lakey also started at sixteen, but he started out as an employee at M.O.R.E., Inc. He was working in our shipping department and eventually migrated over to our printing department, and on the way he started reading the material he was sending out, and started coming up with ideas of his own. **He soon realized just how easy it was to create hot-selling products**. He took that enthusiasm and those ideas, and over the years he worked his way up the company structure -- until nowadays he's writing a lot of the material we send out.

I think the age of sixteen is a defining moment in this business, at least for many of the people I know -- although when I was sixteen, I wasn't interested in writing or anything like that, so I guess I'm the exception. My friend and colleague Mark Nolan, though, was sixteen when he got into the game, too. He noticed a newspaper called MoneysWorth that his parents got in the mail, and saw an ad for the great

Joe Carbo's book "The Lazy Man's Way to Riches." Well, he saved up his money as a dishwasher in a restaurant, and sent off the $10 for Joe's book -- and he tells me that after he read it, he was pretty much ruined for life, as far as doing any hard labor! After moving to Hawaii for a while and starting his writing career penning film reviews, he wrote a book called "Your Ticket to Free Travel" and made a bundle -- and he's just gone forward from there, writing all kinds of newsletters and giving speeches.

Like all the best products, those items were a natural outgrowth of trying to help people, which comes back to the concept of being a good teacher. **If you're trying to help people, the more people you help, the more your reward will be.** So, instead of saying "How can I make money, money, money?" and getting focused on that, think "How can I help the most people?" instead, so you can find a big, profitable market. By asking "How can I help this market in the best way possible?" you'll get the best quality product. By asking, "How can I really do a good job when I help these folks?" you'll keep down your refunds, increase your follow-up orders, and build your loyalty of your customers. <u>Do all that, and the money will follow</u>.

Teaching people this way, helping them acquire the information they want and need, is a great way to make a living. It's not hard labor. It's not like driving a forklift and loading trucks, washing dishes, or being a fry cook. Take it from a man who's done a lot of stuff for a living: nothing is as rewarding as helping people through the information business. **I think once you get into this business and you have a product in mind, it's a lot easier to write a sales letter to sell something than it is to end up writing the product itself.** That's what excites me about the book you're reading today. In the next few chapters, I'm going to teach you secrets you can use to create products easily and simply, even if you think you can't write. These are shortcuts to the writing process, and they can be very effective: I can tell you that from personal experience.

Speaking of personal experience, my wife and I started our own little company back in 1988. She was the president and CEO because she's the responsible business type, and she stayed in that position until just a few years ago, when she had to step down for health reasons. As for me, I just fell in love with the marketing side of the business, so I had a lot to do with producing most of our early products.

We started out with just one product: a little sixteen-page manual. I look at it today and laugh; it's full of typographical errors and the writing is terrible. Unlike Russ, I flunked English all through school; heck, to this day I probably couldn't pass a junior high English test. **English was always my worst subject -- but the fact that I've done so well in the last few decades ought to tell you that <u>the methods I'll outline here</u>, which are used by both me and my closest colleagues, <u>are very effective</u>**.

In any case, we really did get lucky with our first publication, because we were able to sell it for 25-30 times more than it cost us to print it up, and our customers loved it! **This just goes to show that when you've got a great product that people love, you can make an enormous amount of money.** We discovered this by accident, really. We got into this business, placed our initial advertisement for $300 (just about the last money we had), and offered this little manual -- or brochure, really -- to the public. Within a matter of a month after we got started, we were making more money than we had ever made doing anything else -- and we'd tried a whole lot of different things. By then, Eileen and I had tried nine different multi-level marketing companies. We'd had a carpet cleaning business. We were constantly buying get-rich-quick books. They all had some plan for making money, and we were trying all of them. **Finally, we found something that worked.** We wrote a booklet about it, and that was our first project. Who cares if the thing was only sixteen pages long? Who cares if the grammar was atrocious and it was full of typos? <u>It really did help people make money</u>.

To make a long story short, after we'd been in the business about nine months, Russ von Hoelscher came along and started working with us. **Thanks to Russ teaching us a lot of his shortcut strategies, soon we had dozens of products for sale.** It took less than a year before we were working with some of his contacts (particularly the ghostwriters he knew) and were easily producing products based on all of the secrets and shortcuts that he'd taught us. Within four years, we had turned our $300 investment into over $10 million in sales.

Since then, we've done about $100 million more in total sales. We have hundreds -- literally hundreds -- of products available for sale. But we're not that special, really. Yes, we were ambitious; and yes, we wanted to make a lot of money. **But part of the reason we succeeded so well is the simple fact that this is the world's greatest business.** By the time you're done reading this book, you're going to know that. You're going to be so excited when you turn the last page, because you'll realize that this really is the greatest way ever to make money. <u>I truly believe that</u>. One of the reasons we've succeeded as we have is because we've learned many effective shortcut techniques -- the very same ones I'm going to teach you in this book.

Chapter One

"Myth vs. Reality" or "The Need for Speed"

Remember that little sixteen-page booklet I talked about in the introduction, the one with which Eileen and I started our company? That document took us three solid weeks to produce. Nowadays we could do it in three hours. I think a lot of people who are new to the business start out the way we did -- they take forever to get that first product on the market, when it doesn't have to take nearly as long. **The question is, why do they complicate the process so much?**

I think it's partially because most people look at writing as an awesome thing. They may have some favorite authors, or they may be thinking about something like "Gone with the Wind," and they say to themselves, "I could never do that. What talent!" Now, it really does take a little talent to write fiction, because you have to develop a storyline, and you have to have characters, and you have to really work pretty hard at it. **But when it comes to informational products, which is what we're focusing on here, we're talking about simple information.** You can write in simple English, and you don't even have to do it yourself -- like I said earlier, you can get a ghostwriter, usually quite inexpensively. They're always looking for work, and there are just tens of thousands of them out there.

But if you want to do it on your own, and you can speak and write simple English, then go ahead and do it yourself! Get away from the "Gone with the Wind" syndrome that makes you think, "I can't produce a masterpiece." Well, you don't have the leisure to agonize for days about whether to use a comma or a semicolon in a certain passage, like Margaret Mitchell did. You're in this to make money, right? **When you write non-fiction, how-to, moneymaking, or money-saving -- whatever the topic is -- you don't have to be a great storyteller.** You just have to know something about the subject you're discussing. Don't fall into the syndrome of "I can't do it"; because frankly, almost everybody can do it, especially if you use the shortcut methods I'll reveal here.

These shortcut methods are the ABCs to writing good sales copy. Think of it all as a recipe in a cookbook, a formula that lets you do things as simple as 1, 2, 3 -- always assuming you're willing to work at it. That's a key ingredient to any successful recipe; you can't just throw the ingredients together and expect to have a chocolate cake. **It's necessary to put in the elbow grease to mix the ingredients in the proper proportions while seeing to all the details.** If you do that, you're going to end up with a good, edible cake -- or in this case, a sellable, printed product. That may surprise you, but I think that's the challenge that a lot of people have to overcome. They can't get past that block in their own mind saying they can't do this, simply because they don't realize that there are good, effective shortcut secrets to creating printed products.

Get rid of your TV or movie idea of what a writer is or does. In the classic view, the writer cranks that blank page into the typewriter; then he sits there and he's got writer's block for five hours. He types out maybe a sentence, and then he leaves. He comes back the next day and does another sentence. You've seen it a dozen times. **People believe it's an agonizing process that's extraordinarily hard and takes forever, and that it has to be perfect.**

Nothing could be farther from the truth on any of those counts. **Once you put some of these shortcut ideas into effect, you'll change your mind and realize how simple it can be.** Hey, if I can do it, I guarantee that you can! By the time you're done reading this book, you'll be thinking to yourself, "Wow -- there are so many opportunities and so many ideas out there. Let's get started immediately!"

Once again: I think the underlying secret of effectively writing useful, non-fiction stuff if to simply strip away this fiction mystique. When you're writing non-fiction, you just need to do a good job of teaching. So what can you teach? Well, everybody knows something that someone else doesn't know how to do, from how to light a kerosene lantern to how to build a computer. **If you don't know how to do something you want to write about, then you do some research, learn it yourself, or find an expert you can interview.** This is a common practice; a lot of how-to authors and the authors of non-fiction don't necessarily know everything themselves, but they know who to call.

The thing to remember, too, is that if you think there's no way you can possibly learn enough about something (or that you possibly could know enough about one subject to be a teacher and do what I'm talking about here), the reality is that there are always thousands, possibly millions, of people who know a lot less than you do, who would love to learn the few things you do know. So don't ever get caught in a trap of thinking that you don't know enough to write about; you do! If you think otherwise, you're acting as your own worst enemy.

For most of us, our fear of writing begins in school, because that's the only experience that we've had in writing. But, you know, as a little child, you couldn't wait to learn to write. You were writing as soon as you could, having someone show you how to print your name. You wanted to write, and you wanted to create. You went to school and you learned to do that -- and it was fun until someone told you, "Wait a minute. This is the wrong grammar," or "This is the incorrect spelling," or "Your punctuation is wrong." They put those red marks on the paper, and suddenly the process of writing became punishment. What was fun and exciting -- the idea that you could create something on paper -- became just another way for you to be wrong, and no one likes to be wrong! Most of us hate to be judged or criticized, but it happens wherever you are in your career, no matter how popular you may be.

Wayne Dyer is a famous self-help author who once filled Carnegie Hall with people who came just to see him standing up there talking. **His books have all been #1 bestsellers, but people still criticize him.** One guy wrote, "I bought your book for twenty-five cents at a garage sale. I think you personally should send me my twenty-five cents back with an apology." Well, he used to write people like that back and say, "I'm in the smallest room of my house. I have your letter before me, and soon it will be behind me." **Dyer also points out that <u>the only way to avoid criticism is to be nothing, do nothing, and say nothing</u>.** You can do that -- or you can simply decide that you won't let criticism bother you.

So don't make the process it harder than it really is. John Burroughs once said, "The lure of the distant and the difficult is deceptive. The great opportunity is where you are." So, instead of tackling something that's right in front of our faces, something we could do quickly and easily like an audio recording, we think we've got to write the Great American Novel or the most authoritative thousand-page text on the subject -- when we don't. **People want information, and they want it quickly and easily.**

Here's another quote I'd like to share, this time from famous marketer Dan Kennedy: **"What you do doesn't have to be good...just good enough!"** That's another point you should keep in mind. While many of us are perfectionists, that attitude too often complicates every single thing we do. Complicated things don't make you any money; the things that make you money are shortcuts that let you get a product out there very quickly, and then develop a series of those products. Meanwhile, you keep bringing in money from all of the products that you did previously. It's about as simple as that. Forget about the hard way. Forget about staring at blank paper and saying to yourself, "Oh, dear, what can I do?" **I'm going to show you how to get started quickly.**

Another thing: something I've noticed about all the hundreds of projects that I've worked on is that once you start, you're half done. By that, I mean we over-think things too often. Sometimes we try to make something difficult, even when it's really simple -- and even when we know it's simple. I don't know why this is; maybe it's just human nature. But in my case, I've found that as soon as I force myself to write the first page (and often I do have to force myself!), I'm half done. From then on, it just starts to flow.

Remember, with the methods that I'm going to show you, you don't have to be a writer at all; you don't have to be a recognized expert, and best of all, you don't need a lot of money to invest. You can get started with pocket change. You can be on your way to making a nice profit very, very quickly.

By the end of this book, I guarantee you: you're going to realize this is the world's greatest way to make money, and you'll know the shortcuts to getting a quick start and raking in the cash.

Chapter Two

It's All About Communication

My next secret is one that's been beloved by editors and publishers for centuries: the press release. Press releases are everywhere. **Every company known to man is constantly releasing press releases packed with information, facts, and late-breaking news about new products, new services, and new information.** Well, guess what? The neat thing about a press release is it's for release. It's there for you to use word for word, if you want. This is the one situation where you can literally pick out whole chunks or entire documents and reuse them at will, and you'll get patted on the back for doing so. **Make the proper use of existing press releases, and bingo: you'll appear to be very knowledgeable.** After all, you're bringing this information to the reader, and they're happy to have it. The wonderful news is that, on the Internet, there are thousands of press releases released every day.

One of the best products to put together with press releases is a product directory. To put one together this quickly, just go to any search engine on the Internet, and type in the keyword of the subject you want to write about. **For example, if you're interested in horses, horse racing, auto racing, cameras, or photography, you enter in the appropriate keyword and bang! You'll find hundreds and hundreds of websites from companies that supply these types of products and services.** You can go to each of these sites, and you'll find that most offer an area for the press to go to. This is where they keep their latest press releases, which you can grab and use at will. There's also almost always a place where you can leave your email or snail mail address and get on their press release list -- which means you don't have to ever go back to these people to get the newest news. You can start receiving tons of information in your mailbox, and then just start putting together either newsletters or product directories that way.

Another great place to go is to a site like **www.prnewswire.com**, **www.prweb.com**, or **www.ereleases.com**. These sites all offer links where you can sign up to receive press releases -- and you can even pick specific categories about which you want to hear. You can also pluck press releases from lists of today's news or last week's news. Interestingly enough, each of these websites is anxious to get the press releases to you. They want people to send them press releases, too, because they make their money by charging these companies to distribute their press releases and get them into as many hands as possible. On your end, it's free to sign up and receive this information.

My good friend and colleague Alan Bechtold has used this technique to publish trade journals that have made him a very good living in the online industry. He's published computer news magazines for video gamers using this technique, not to mention countless other products and services. **He's made a great living by just being the editor and publisher, and never really having to write a word** -- he just finds news that he thinks would interest his readers, and edits it down into a shortcut form so it's a little more readable.

So without writing anything, you can produce valuable documents. The neat thing about a product directory is you can use this technique to create a directory that goes into facts and figures about the product, taking advantage of white papers that they've issued with their press releases that detail how the product was developed and why it's so valuable or why it stands out above the competitors. So, provide more information than just a list of products, their prices, and who to contact, and remember -- product directories do get outdated, so you've got a product that you need to come back and update once a year, twice a year, or quarterly. **Now you've got a product that you can update, just by using those press releases that are pouring into your mailbox, and re-release regularly to make more money with it.** It's an incredible way to get established in an industry. At some point, you become an expert, so now you can write your own products and establish your own special niche.

Most modern publications rely on press releases very heavily; in fact, most publications you read on the newsstand are put together in just the way I've described. Why? Because of one thing: downsizing. Publications all over the world are cutting their staffs due to increasing costs, so press releases are very important.

Installment Writing

Here's another great shortcut secret: writing on the installment plan. When we make purchases, most of us buy on the installment plan, because it lets us get the fun part now and delay the pain -- the payment -- by spreading it out to make it as painless as possible. We do that for most high-ticket items, whether we're buying cars, televisions, or computers. **What I'm going to share with you is a way to create a product that reverses that process.** You get paid now, and spread the writing out over time.

Here's how it works. First of all, decide on the product that you want to create, the subject, and the price. Then, create your ad or sales letter. If you go with a sales letter, create one with a lot of bullet points. **If you don't already know, bullet points are strong sales points that are brief and succinct -- usually one-liners headed by a dot, or in printing terms, a "bullet."** They tease you and make you want to know; they challenge you, and make you guess whether you know the answer or not. So create a sales letter that's filled with bullet points, and offer your customer the chance to read over your shoulder as you create this new product.

Everyone wants information before anyone else gets it; everyone likes to be on the inside. **This gives them a chance to do just that, because what they're going to do is buy your publication now and get the publication in installments over the next few months as you create it.** They get a sneak peek, so to speak; they're invited to make their comments and offer feedback as you create this project. Let's say your product was originally set to sell for $99. You can go two ways with this, or use a combination of both. Suppose you offer the product to these sneak peek customers at $99 with a very exciting bonus attached, or you discount the price and offer a $99 product to them for $75 on the sneak-peek plan. You can still include your bonus if you want to; remember, it's just information. **It's not going to cost you any more money to do it this way**.

Once you've completed your sales letter and have your basic offer to post on your website, or to send out by direct mail if you're using mail order, write your first chapter or section of your product. **Now, it doesn't have to be more than ten or twelve pages, but you want to make certain that you absolutely <u>pack</u> it with information**. Take your time in creating it, as much time as you need, but make it good. After you write a section, read it out loud to be certain it reads well. Don't make it sound like an introduction to a book or a manual, something that tells you the history of the product and what you're going to talk about; **give them a lot of useful information, because this is the first piece of material your sneak-peek customer is going to receive -- and you want to impress them**.

As soon as a prospect decides to become a sneak-peek customer, he can obtain the first section of the product. If you're going the Internet route, he can download it directly from your website. Then, each month (or six weeks, or whatever schedule you set up in the beginning), you'll create a new section of your product, and you'll email it to that customer. **You invite them to make their comments on the product as you go**. Some won't, but it's amazing how many people will give you feedback. You now have all the money up front; you have their money in your bank, so you're now writing on a leisurely basis. Remember, though, you do have to write on that schedule you've set; but that's okay. You have a direction to go; you have all those bullet points to follow.

And you have that feedback coming in from your customers, to make the process easier. Some will email you suggestions or stories you can use; some will do free research for you, and tell you things you didn't already know. You'll also have an editorial staff, because if you make any mistakes, grammatical or proofreading, you can be sure someone will call it to your attention! **In a way, then, they're doing much of the work for you for free.** And remember, sending your updates by email isn't costing you a penny. There's no invoicing, there's no packing, there's no postage. It's not adding to your cost of this product at all.

Then, when you finish the final section and send it out, you can finish up by sending the customers a final copy of the product -- in hardcopy, if you care to, or you can let them download the complete, revised product off the Web. **This creates a very loyal customer, because they're involved and invested in the creation process, and end up with a valuable product that's theirs in more ways than one.** It makes your writing painless, since you're writing just a little each month over the period of months -- and you had all the money up front while you were being paid to write the product. It's instant profit, and that makes writing a financial pleasure.

Simplify!

This next idea deals with trying to make the entire product-creation process as simple as possible. Earlier, I talked about how most people have the perception that writing is difficult. **Well, one of the shortcuts that works best for me is when I don't have to write anything -- when everything's done for me.** One of the best self-published products that I can think of where that's the case is the compilation of real-life stories and samples.

Let me give you an example. A couple of years ago, when my friend Jeff Gardner's wife was trying to create a resume to get a job as a veterinarian, she and Jeff went to the bookstore and found literally dozens of books on how to write a resume. These things were huge, and you had to read the whole thing just to figure out how the heck to write the thing. **Well, they came upon a book that was just 100-150 pages long -- but instead of teaching you how to write a resume, it offered examples of actual resumes, one after the other, grouped into different categories depending on the type of job.** Whether you were trying to be an airline pilot, an IRS agent, or a veterinarian, inside was a real-life resume that you could use as an example to create your own. Of course, Jeff and his wife bought that book, because it made the process very simple.

I've noticed that a lot of companies do the exact same thing. There's a company that offers a book that's full of actual business letters, so that if you need to write a certain type of letter -- say, a collection letter -- you can flip to page 243, see how someone else wrote one, and write yours along those same lines. In a similar vein, you can create a compilation of all sorts of business forms, and sell that to businesses. **There are also marketing companies that have put together compilations of sales letters, because people are always interested in how somebody else sold a particular product -- what type of guarantee they offered, what bullet points they emphasized, or what type of pricing they used.** Having a compilation of sales letters from other companies, especially if they're successful sales letters, really helps. Those types of products sell very well.

Another example I'd like to give of somebody using this idea comes from one of my friends, Mark Nolan. Mark Nolan is known as the "king of press releases," and he specializes in helping people get free advertising through them. One of the best ways to learn how to write press releases is to actually look at real life examples that have helped people get free advertising, so he put together a compilation of a whole series of successful press releases. **The best thing about this idea, as I've already mentioned, is that because you're compiling something that's already been written, and is already in use, you're not having to write this yourself.** You can use this concept with almost any niche.

Back to the Basics

If you don't mind doing some writing yourself, this next idea is very effective. **I want to discuss the basics of how to quickly write a book, because if I can show you how to do that, then writing a report, a booklet, or a manual will be a cinch.** But before I do that, let's take a look at what's selling well in book form right now. What are the million-dollar topics with which you can make the most money? Here's a list of ten that I've compiled:

1. Moneymaking information
2. Money-saving information
3. Good how-to information
4. Health information
5. Computers
6. Information for senior citizens
7. Gambling
8. Personal relationships
9. Investment information
10. The unusual (UFOs, ESP, etc)

Of course, there are many more topics with which you can make money, but give these ten some consideration, because they're <u>literally</u> million-dollar topics.

Now, I want to discuss very briefly how to write a full-length book -- because like I said, if you can do that, you can do anything, as long as you pick a decent topic. Make sure you do your research, and know there's a market for your topic before you start. That's something you should always do first. Then, write your ad or sales letter, or both, and also the table of contents for your book. Fill it with benefits. Even before you start writing, you want to know what you're going to put in it, because as with the serial project I mentioned earlier in the chapter, this will help you write it. Once you have the advertising material, you then have to put in the book every benefit that you mentioned in your ad.

Next, start gathering material. Go to the library, or better yet, go to the Internet -- you'll find ten times more data. I don't care what the topic is, you can go to the search engines and find more about that topic than you ever wanted to know. **Between the library and the search engines, you're going to have all the reference material you could ever want.** Next, decide on the number of chapters and their headings, then set up legal-size folders for every chapter. Start putting the reference material that you've gathered into the proper folders, and continue to do that until, in your judgment, you have enough to create a decent chapter. You'll be amazed at how quickly you amass data, if you just keep at it. Once you've done that, you have the ad, the sales letter, you've done the table of contents, and you've got your folders full of the chapter material. At that point, it's going to be relatively simple for you to write that book over the next few months.

Say It Without Writing a Word

If the process described above sounds like too much work, then here's another simple way to create a product without having to write anything -- assuming you pick the right topic. **Instead of putting something together yourself, go find an expert and let them write the words for you.** Now, I'm not talking about having them write the book for you, although that's always a possibility. What I'm talking about is finding a public speaker, someone who speaks on a topic that interests you or a topic that you believe interests a lot of other people are interested in, and

---

getting permission from them to transcribe their speech and turn it into a manual. Now, maybe they'll say, "Sure. I have no interest in writing, and I'll let you do it for free," or maybe they'll want a cut of the profits. Either way, you can work out some kind of arrangement easily enough. **You'd be surprised how many speakers are flattered that you would even be interested in their speech, and that you thought their speech was good enough to turn into a manual.** A lot of public speakers, you'll find, aren't interested in writing at all. They may have no desire to turn their speech into a book, so that gives you an opportunity to profit. The transcription process itself is relatively simple. If you don't want to hire out the actual transcription -- which is generally pretty inexpensive -- then do it yourself. You can buy recording equipment that lets you use a foot pedal to start and pause a tape as you need to. When you're done, you just need to clean up the text and have a typesetter make it look nice. That's easy to do.

Here's another thing you might try. **Maybe a half-hour speech wouldn't translate into a very big manual -- so instead, you find four or five speakers, and compile their best speeches into a manual that might be 200-300 pages long, or even a book with three to four different sections, each section by a different speaker.** Another thing you can do: if you can't find an expert who's already giving speeches, find an expert and interview them yourself. Prepare lots of questions that you know your customers would love to know the answers to, then sit down with a tape recorder and chat with them face-to-face. Once that's done, you can transcribe that interview, or you can sell the audio recordings directly -- or both. That's worked very well for Eileen and I. In fact, we once interviewed Russ von Hoelscher over the course of a weekend, paying him his standard $2,500 fee. The resulting product did $1.3 million in sales, so as you can see, it's an excellent way to create products without having to write a word. You never have to stare at a blank page!

Eh, Why Bother?

Here's a point I wanted to bring up about selling a product on the Internet, using research you've collected from that very source, and why it's such a good way to make a nice stack of money with a minimum of work. By now, you've probably twigged to the fact that this is a kind of a "Catch-22". After all, you're basing the product on information that's available to anyone with an Internet connection. **So why would people go onto the Internet and buy it from you? Why don't they just go and collect it themselves?**

For the same reason that only five people out of one hundred -- only 5% of the population of the United States, the most highly-educated country in the history of the world -- have a library card. The library is completely filed with books, magazines, and newspapers from all over the world, free of charge. You can check them out and take them home for weeks at a time, or you can read them there. You can access the Internet at the library and find everything you're looking for, or you can just go up to the reference desk and ask. But only five out of one hundred people ever bother. So, when most people get a sales letter in the mail from me that says, "I'd be happy to share this information with you, all collected in one place. It's very painless. All you do is give me your credit card number, and I'll give it to you," they say, "You bet!"

That's because you're doing them a service. More than ever before, time is money. Most people don't have the time to do their own research, or they won't make the time.

They're home watching television instead of going to the library, because they're tired after a long day of work. They don't see any adventure in it, like I do. I love to find out new stuff. It's kind of like being an antique shopper: you can't pass an antique store if you're an antique maniac. Well, an information merchant like me can't drive by a bookstore, a library, or go on the Internet without stopping and looking at all the wonders there. We just love information. We're information junkies.

That's why you can go on the Internet and find the information, collect it all in one place very quickly, edit it, and have a viable product. **Instead of trying to find a product and then hoping someone will buy it, find a huge group of people who are already saying, "I want this, I want this," and give it to them.** It's like fishing. If you fish in a puddle, there's a chance there might be one minnow in there; but if you go into the ocean, there are tons of fish to catch. You just throw out your net and reel it in. So, let's go where the customers are. Let's follow the consumer trends.

Last year, more than 60 million Americans used the Internet. **According to the polling firm Lou Harris and Associates, a large percentage of those people, about 68%, looked for some kind of health or medical information at least once -- <u>so there's a big market right there.</u>** Health is huge; it's a hot topic. Sure, some of these folks are cybercondriacs, which is a funny new word they've come up with; every day they wonder if they've got some new disease. They're the same people that buy all those health books through the mail -- and now they're going online and they're searching for information. They're flocking by the tens of thousands to these health information sites.

In response, my colleague Mark Nolan put up a web site offering a health book called "Health Secrets of the Rich and Famous." It had a little bit of pizzazz, kind of a show-biz angle to it, and chronicled what people in Hollywood, famous politicians, and similar folks do to stay healthy. These are people who have unlimited amounts of money, who will spend anything to stay young, and whose health directly affects their performance and the money that they make. That book sold like hotcakes.

The way you can come up with a book like this is to go online and start searching for health sites; there are thousands of them. For example, there's one specialty medical information site called "Medline." **Recently, their online stats went from 7 million searches to over 120 million in a year.** I'd say that's definitely a "gold rush." About a third of those searches were done by consumers -- not doctors, nurses, or any other health care professionals. Forty million consumers. That's a lot of customers looking for information that you could sell.

A lot of these sites steer people to a hospital site, a pharmacy board, or something similar. **You don't want to provide too much detailed information on your site, because some sites have recently come under scrutiny from state medical boards for practicing what's called "virtual medicine" without a license.** So, be careful what you say on there. You know better than to give medical advice anyway. Just set up a gateway or portal to sites your users will find useful. For example there's a great government site, provided by the Department of Health and Human Services, that's called healthfinder.gov. It offers over 1,000 topics and links to government and non-profit content, all checked for quality. **You can do something similar. If you have a gateway site, all of a sudden you have an information product.** All your information is in the links to these other sites. You're one-stop shopping. They come to your site, and though you don't have anything for sale, they see all these handy links. They can go anywhere they want, but you're the hub.

So, how do you make money this way? <u>You sell advertising to all those sites to which you are the gateway</u>. What if you had 120 million visitors a year, like Medline? Heck, what if you had half that? Even if you don't actively seek advertising sources, there are people that will come to you and say, "We see you're getting all these visitors, so we want to put an ad on your site," and you say, "Great!" You get your head webgeek pilot to put their ad or banner on the site, then proceed to you collect money. It's easy -- you're selling electrons. You have no fulfillment, no shipping, no packaging, no printing, no writing, no recording, nothing like that to worry about. There's no cost of duplication. There's no postage. Your product can be up in just a day or two if you are setting up a site like this and put all these links on it.

Just find something everybody wants to know about. Search the Internet, collect the sites that you think are best, and put them all on one page. Call it a hub, a link site, or a gateway. Make it attractive, but not too flashy. Then when people search for that topic, you'll rise in the search engines, since you've got all those sites listed in one spot.

The Firstest with the Mostest

People frequently come up to Eileen and I and ask us, "How in the world do you produce so many of these products?" I'd specifically like to address that issue, and talk about some of the best informational products that Eileen and I sell. **Now, when I say best, I'm talking about the fastest -- so I've got a list of five of the best and fastest kinds of products that we've produced here at M.O.R.E., Incorporated.**

Although the title of this book is "Shortcut Secrets to Making High Profit Products," you need to realize that there are all kinds of different informational products you can create, and sell at anywhere from ten to thirty times -- or more! -- than your actual costs to produce them. The fact that the customers get excellent value is very important, too, since the whole idea is to give your customers so much value they'll want to come back for more.

The top product class on our list of five is books and manuals -- no surprise there, right? Years ago, Russ von Hoelscher taught us how to use ghostwriters, and since then we've had ghostwriters create dozens of different books for us. All we do, at most, is give them the research materials -- and sometimes they go out and get their own. Then they do all the work of writing, too. **Because it's a project for hire, once they turn it in we pay them, and then we put our name on it and sell it.** We keep all the profits. You can do this, too! Here's something else you can do safely, once you own the copy: you can use the same chapters over again, as necessary, in several books -- and you can find new ways to use those same chapters in other manuals, simply through rewriting. You can rewrite the material a little bit, or you can build a manual or book very easily by simply reusing things that you've done in other manuals -- as long as the customer gets good value. Remember, that's the key secret. **The only real difference between a manual and a book is the binding.** If you put it in a three-ring binder, you'd call it a manual; if you have it perfect bound, you'd call it a book. So, don't get hung up on the terms here.

The second product on our list is home study courses. This is where you package up a ton of stuff and sell it as a batch: for example, a mix of videos, audiocassettes, reports, back issues of newsletters, tip sheets. What you're really shooting for here is for the customer to open it up when they get it, and it's like Christmastime. There's a huge amount of stuff that jumps out at them -- so much that they don't know what to do first. **The benefit of selling home study courses is that you can turn $50 worth of hard costs into $500 or $800 easily by selling it as a package containing different informational products that are grouped together under a main theme.** Now, admittedly, it's got to be a hot subject -- 101 Ways to Mow Your Lawn isn't going to cut it. But pick one of the hot topics I've talked about earlier, and you can instantly get ten to twenty times your basic cost just by packaging it all up like this.

The third thing on our list is recorded seminars. Let's say you have a live seminar for your customers, your prospects, or your clients; be sure you record it, so you can then simply sell the audiotapes, videotapes, or printed transcripts of that seminar in pieces or as a whole. This is something that has a tremendous value; some of our seminars have sold for $5,000 or more, so when we package those seminars and sell the transcripts, they have a high perceived value. **That's a great way that we can sell something for ten to thirty times what it costs us to produce.**

Number four is newsletters. We like newsletters, because of the commitment that it takes to do a newsletter every month. It does force you to do something, and continue to produce something useful. **Then, here's the beautiful part: not only are you getting paid by the subscribers as you're producing the newsletter, later on you can sell back issues of those newsletters, all packaged up.** You make money two ways, so that's a very popular product for us.

Number five is multi-author products. Russ von Hoelscher is the one who first taught us how to do this; in fact, as I pointed out earlier, one of the first products we did with Russ was a simple round table discussion. **We just sat around the table with microphones and interviewed Russ. Since then we've done that a lot, and in fact we've put together so many products with other people that the work we've had to do is minimal.** That's what we do every week now, in fact: we get together with a group of people who all have customers and clients who want the same type of materials and information, and we spend a couple hours a week putting together two 45-minute audio recordings. Every week! It really adds up after a while; in fact, after four sessions, you're able to produce a 150-170 page manual. Plus, you have eight 45-minute recordings. That's a product that can and does easily sell for $150 to $195.

So there you have it: when you can, get other people to do the work. There are so many people out there who have good products, and there's no reason not to get them to joint venture with you or to do the interviews that we talked about. Use other people's talent and brains to create your own product. It's so simple. You ask questions and record the answer. Who would have thought that we would have raked in over a million dollars, when we were just sitting at the dining room table recording that one product with Russ all those years ago? It just shows you the power of information, and how simple it is to produce, and how much money you can make. **You can literally become a millionaire by doing very little work -- <u>as long as you're providing real value to the customer</u>.** That's the kicker. It has to be worth something to them, so don't expect to sell Aunt Hilda Mae's pickle recipes effectively this way. Of course, you have to remember that whatever you produce, there will always be people who will perceive it as junk. We get this reaction even from some of our relatives, even $100 million later; they think some of the stuff Eileen and I publish is garbage, because they're not in the market. But obviously, it's not. **This just shows that they don't understand for whom these products and publications were developed.** Even if they think that some of our stuff is pure garbage, the truth is that our customers love it.

You know, it's difficult to explain what you do in this business. People are constantly asking us, "What in the heck do you do?" and we say, "We sell information." "Well, what kind of information?" "Information that people want to buy." And that's the long and the short of it. We don't worry about whether that information's in book form, manual form, audio recording, or whatever. **It's just information...and as long as it's valuable, you'll make money on it.** If I write on an old, stained cocktail napkin a secret about how you can make a thousand dollars, guaranteed, in twenty-four hours, that cocktail napkin and ink might be worth a couple cents -- but the information printed on it is still worth $1,000. **That's what people pay for: the information, not how it's presented.** Whatever format you put it in, just remember, you've got to deliver that high-quality information.

It's that easy. Most people who try this business focus on the process of writing and make it a barrier. They focus on how difficult it's going to be, or the fact that they've never done it before. That shouldn't be the focus; the focus should be on the quality of information, not the form that it takes. **Success lies in really helping people, in trying to reach out and communicate.** As the old saying goes: Give a man a fish, and he'll eat for a day; teach him to fish, and he'll eat for life.

Chapter Three

Tap Into Your Creativity

When you're looking for shortcuts to creating informational products that you can sell for many years, you need to dig deep into your personal stock of creativity to find the best ideas. And don't tell me you don't have any -- we all do, especially those of us audacious enough to become entrepreneurs, to work for ourselves on our own terms. For example, here's a creative technique that's been used by publishers large and small, in every kind of industry or specialty out there, for many years. The publishers of "Chicken Soup for the Soul" even used this technique to create millions of dollars' worth of information and entertainment products. **Whatever topic you're covering, just set up a contest seeking the best tips, tricks, how-to's, and such.** Some of the topics that would work in any area of selling and marketing would be crafts or relationships. You could create a product called, "How I Met My Wife and Got Her to Say Yes," then just seek people's best true personal stories relating to that.

With a contest, you always think prizes. If you have the cash, you can offer a cash prize for the Number One tip or trick. This is different from what I talked about earlier. There are some people out there who offer prizes for the best writing quality or best style, and sometimes you have to be qualified to judge that kind of thing. **But for selling and marketing, crafts, or relationships, especially non-fiction (informational) topics, you really only have to pick the tip, trick, how-to, or personal story you liked the best.** Make it clear that you're going to pick the one that you like the best, as editor, and give that one the First Prize. The next five get runner-up prizes or whatever. Then, you don't have to be qualified to judge the quality of the writing.

If you don't have cash, here's another idea: **you could call companies related to the topic of the tips you're gathering**. For example, in crafts such as glassmaking, you could call companies that sell supplies or glass itself to people who do stained glass work. Tell them you're doing a book on that, then get one or more of those companies to put up either products or services as prizes in return for a sponsorship position in the books. **Maybe give them a page in the book for an ad, a four-page catalog, or whatever it takes to trade to get free prizes for your top five people.** Of course, you would also mention them as the sponsors that made this contest possible in all of your promotional materials, and anything else you do to promote and attract people to send you these materials.

When it comes to announcing to the world that you've got this contest going, here comes the Internet again. **Use Internet newsgroups for advertising; it's the best way I can imagine to inexpensively attract people who will give you their stories and ideas right online or by email, so you don't even have to retype them to put them in the book.** You could just post a message on any of the newsgroups that relate to the interest area you're covering. There are newsgroups out there for anything. You could leave a message like, "I'm writing a book and need your help." I would suggest you state it that way rather than as a strict contest, because this gives it more of a "gosh, wow" factor. **The readers think, "Neat! He's a writer, and I want to help him out."** For example, you can say something like: "I'm looking for true stories of outdoor survival, detailing how you got through the experience step-by-step, 100-250 words long. The best five will get survival gear free from XYZ Company." You can bet people will respond quickly.

If you don't have any money or sponsors, offer the book itself free to the top five winners, or even to everyone you publish. **If you offer a book free to everyone you publish, you'd still sell a bunch more of those books to the people buying them for their friends, family, and the like.** And that's another thing, one of the neatest things about this technique for building an information product: you develop a ready market for the book just by asking for these stories. <u>Everybody who submits, whether they get accepted or not, is a potential buyer of the book</u>. If you make them a special discount offer because they submitted to you, they'll buy the book in quantity. So with this method, you've got a ready, built-in market, and it's a great way to put together top-flight products with interesting stories and information that you couldn't possibly dig up yourself.

Chat With the Experts

Here's an extension of that last idea: get the most successful, most visible people on the Internet to write your product for you. You can profit from their work in two ways. First of all, if they're going to write the book for you, you need to know what's going to be in the book. So, you need to sit down and make a list of the topic areas you want to cover in your book. Let's say you're going to show people how to put together a website and pick a hosting company. They may need to have someone design their site for them. If so, they're going to need a website designer, a marketing consultant, auto responders… go right down the list of the things that any successful website that makes money would have. Those will be your chapters or sections.

Now, you look for someone in each of those product areas that is likely to write a section for you. **You begin at your computer with your search engines.** If you're starting with hosting companies, you look up the different companies available, and pick a few that you think are good prospects. Contact the first one; if that doesn't work, go down your list. Basically, you've got an offer to make these suppliers that they really can't refuse. You're going to offer them credibility and visibility, and you're going to help them build traffic to their website. That's a pretty powerful offer. **What they're going to do for you in return is give you ten to twelve pages on the topic area that you assign them.** In other words, you're going to contact a hosting company and ask them to write ten to twelve pages about how to find a host, what a host does for you, and explain the terms and fundamentals of hosting. **In return for those pages, they become a published author. That gives them credibility. Since you're going to sell a lot of copies of your book, that gives them visibility.**

Doing this, you can find ten to fifteen topics very easily. **That gives you a book of 120 pages or more, a nice, solid product drawn from people who are writing from their own experience that you can sell at a good price.** The reason they're probably going to agree to do this is because most of them already have some of this material prepared. So, it's a win-win situation. They can let you have the material with very little new work. All you're left to do is write an introduction that ties the pieces together.

This can build traffic to their website, too. Just ask each of the people who participates to do one other task: to post a checklist on their website that provides the steps to finding a host that meets your needs, or the ten pitfalls to finding a host or website designer, or the ten mistakes commonly made in selecting a host or web designer. In each section that they've written, they give their website address and offer the checklist. What this does is bring people to their site to read the book. It also brings the reader to the site to get the checklist, which they can then print out. It keeps the material current, and the writer of each section can also make a special offer to acquire customers. The hosting service, for instance, can say, "We'll give you thirty days at no cost." **So you give him traffic, a chance to make an offer to a customer, credibility, and visibility.** It's a combination on which you just can't lose.

I said there was a second way you could profit, and here it is: **you sell the reprint rights to this product.** Let's say you sell some of the rights to interested websites to reprint and sell as many of these publications as they like, and you charge them $500. If you find fifty people who would like to buy that, there's an extra $25,000 -- and all this from writing done for you by other people. I don't think you can beat that combination.

Superfast Product Creation

This is the perfect lead-in to my next point, which is this: what if your lead time is remarkably short? **What if you needed to create a product within 24 hours? Well, you can do that too! You can have a complete product, already put together, typeset completely, in less than a day.** Not just a complete product, but a product that's been completely proven and that comes complete with sales material to help sell it. How do you do that? Easy! **You buy the reprint rights for an existing product, just like I mentioned in the previous section.** There are so many companies out there right now that have sold a product and made $100,000, $500,000, even a million dollars with it -- and now they're ready to sell you the reprint rights. You should take advantage of the opportunity, because it quickly gives you a proven product that's already been tested. You can immediately start promoting it on your own.

You don't have to promote it exactly the way you buy it. **In many cases, you can go back into that product and change it around, reformat it, give it a new cover, change the title, and perk it up so it actually stands out a little bit and it doesn't sound like the same old, same old.** All these are easy things you can do to very quickly make the product your own, and separate it from what's been sold previously. Plus, you can take some reports from other authors, or some audio recordings and videos you may have either created yourself or bought reprint rights to, add that all together -- and suddenly you have a home study course or package deal, a bigger product that you can sell for $500, $1,000, or $2,000.

Many information marketers actually prefer doing this, versus having a ghostwriter create a product from scratch. There's absolutely nothing wrong with having something ghostwritten; after all, it's a shortcut. **You can find ghostwriters in some of the writing magazines, like Writer's Digest, or on freelancer sites like Elance.com.** You give them the topic and maybe some research materials, and they'll write the information for you. **The challenge of doing it that way is two-fold, though. You've got to pay them a pretty good amount per page: it can be anywhere from $15 and up per double-spaced page.** If you want a 100-200 page product that's single-spaced and in small type, you might have to request 350-400 pages from your ghostwriter -- and if you're paying $15 a page, that adds up pretty quickly. Plus, you're getting an unproven product with no sales material.

So if you want a quick product that's proven to work, you should definitely think about looking at some of the reprint rights offers that are out there. There are quite a few, and more are coming out all the time. Just keep your eyes open. **Remember, you don't have to sell exactly what everybody else is selling. You can just make a few changes -- very easy changes -- to a reprint rights package you purchase, and instantly, you have something that's your own.** Sure, it's not brand new, but it's new to your customers. You can go out there, sell it, and make another $100,000, $500,000, or even $1 million with that product. It's very fast, very simple, very effective -- and can be very, very profitable.

Multiple Streams of Income

You know, most of us in the business think of our products in terms of a book or maybe a computer diskette, a CD, or cassette tapes, but we don't see the whole picture. For example, Eileen and I have buckets and boxes full of recordings of tele-seminars and conference calls that we've done in years gone by that we haven't always done much with, and I know this is true of other people in our field as well. To our credit, I think, Eileen and I have been having the tapes transcribed for quite some time, and recently we've been going back and turning them into publications; this is just one example.

But many people in the field stick with audio recordings of one kind or another, and don't take it any further. They think that's the best way to go -- and maybe for them, it is. Well, why not approach these people with a deal? Tell them you like their recordings, and that you'd like to transcribe these tapes into the printed word, if they'll let you sell them. Once you've transcribed it, you'll give them a copy and they can sell it too. You may have to pay something for some of the titles, but some you might just get for doing the work. **The point is, there are so many products out there that have only been done one way -- which offers you a fantastic way to make money.**

That's because the best way to make money in the information business and in self-publishing is to consider multiple steams of income. You write an article, or you buy an article, then you turn it into a report. If you get enough reports together, you turn it into a book, cassette tapes, CDs, CD-ROMS, and the like -- all the same product, but in different forms. Thousands of articles are appearing on the Internet and in various magazines every day that you can use. Let's say you want to do a book on home business; well, there are thousands of articles in print and on the Internet about home business. **So my suggestion would be that you get in touch with the writer or publisher -- they're sometimes the same person, especially on the 'Net -- and tell them you want to do a book on home business.** Tell them, for example, "Hey, I loved your article that just appeared in Spare Time magazine, and I'd like permission to reprint it. In return, I'll send you a copy of the book when it comes out, plus I'll give you a deeply discounted price on the book, if you want to buy it and sell it yourself." A lot of authors of are going to say "Sure!" Once you have a bunch of these articles and put together your book for sale, you go back to the people and say, "Hey, now I want to create a CD-ROM! You'll get the rights to sell the CD-ROM at a super price."

This is something that Russ von Hoelscher teaches, and I think it's a great way to think outside the box and take advantage of all the audio products out there that no one has ever really done anything with. A few years back, Russ was talking to a client of his who produces tons of motivational tapes and he said to her, "You know, you should transcribe some of these and make them into manuals." It turns out that she'd never thought of that. She'd done about a hundred motivational tapes by then, and she'd bought rights to other people's tapes, but had never considered any other way to handle the products. Don't let that opportunity pass you by!

In a similar vein, don't forget about the opposite situation. **A lot of people have printed matter that they could actually take and turn into an audio recording; you can do that also.** If you have a book or manual, basically all you have to do is take the highlights of it, turn it into a script, and record yourself verbally going over the same information that you've printed in the book.

Listen to Expert Advice

Here's a simple idea, but in practice it works very well -- as we've proven in the past. I discussed it in Chapter 2, but I think it bears repeating. **Here's the secret: record someone else giving advice.** Previously, I talked about how, years back, Eileen and I paid Russ to come out and spend a weekend with us. We basically hammered him with questions and spent the whole weekend, several hours a day, picking his brain -- asking him every kind of question related to making money in information publishing that we could think of. We used that to produce an audio program called the "$2,500 Weekend Package," because $2,500 was what we paid Russ to come out for the weekend. Our customers just loved that, because most of them -- and I'm talking about thousands of people here -- couldn't afford to actually hire Russ and pay him $2,500 to come to their house to spend the weekend with them. But hey -- they could afford the $195 we charged for an audio program where they got the same information they could have paid $2,500 for in a more complex form -- and they didn't have to put Russ up in their house, or pay for a hotel room for him for the weekend. They just got to pop in an audiocassette and listen to him reveal his greatest secrets for making big money in mail order.

This is something you can do whether you're in the mail order business or have any other kind of product you'd like to sell. **Get someone in your field to sit down and talk; you don't even have to have them come out and spend a weekend with you.** You can do it over the telephone, just interview them and record it, asking them all kinds of questions that you can think of. The most important thing to remember is to ask them questions that you know your customers are interested in learning the answers to. You can create a one-hour program, a two-hour program, three, four, eight; it doesn't matter how much. The important thing is to keep it interesting. You can even interview a dozen experts in your field, and offer a big home study package that you can can sell for $495 or even more, assuming you provide lots of information in an interesting field.

Here's another good example of a company that has effectively used shortcut techniques, like the ones I'm discussing here, to make a pile of money: Reiman Publications. They publish about ten different magazines, including <u>Country Magazine</u> and <u>Birds and Blooms</u>. They have millions and millions of readers. I know that because I checked up on their mailing list; like most big companies, their list is available for rental to direct mail merchandisers. **It's a massive database, and what makes it especially interesting is that the people on the list are the same people who supply a lot of the content of the magazines.** Every month, people send their country photographs into <u>Country Magazine</u>, which they advertise as "for everyone who lives in or longs for the country" (I subscribe myself). It's filled with beautiful, full-color photos of the outdoors, kids, wildlife, pet pigs, you name it. It's kind of corny, and everyone just loves it. One of their most famous pictures -- you've probably seen it as a poster -- is of a couple of kids wearing bib overalls with a caption under it saying, "Been farming long?" The point is, all the photos come from the readers. They send in the photos, then they pay the company to look at them -- so it's an easy job for <u>Country Magazine</u>.

The cooking magazines -- and they have several -- are basically recipes. People send in their favorite country recipes for biscuits, cornbread, the chili recipe that won a contest at their State Fair, along with a photo -- and the magazine runs the recipes the readers send in. And then, of course, the readers pay to read the other readers' recipes. **So these guys really don't have a lot of writing to do. All their material comes in the mail.** Then, when they've published a few magazine issues, they put it all in a book, and viola: they have a book of recipes, and everyone buys that collection, too.

That's a great and very effective shortcut: have your public submit the stuff that you sell back to them. First of all, they're happy to see their own photo or recipe in print. Second of all, they love to read what all the other guys have sent in. You can also do this on the Internet. **Here's one example: one fellow ran a discussion board about marketing, the business, and the Internet -- he'd answer any questions on the subject anyone asked -- and one of his participants asked him for permission to take all the most interesting questions the man had answered and puts them in a printed book.** The guy said, "Sure, as long as I can have the rights to it also." So they went through the discussion board and picked out all the best questions and answers: How do I get a merchant account? How do I get this printed cheap? Where can I find a good mailing list company? They put them all together, and they had an instant booklet. It took the guy one day to do it.

There are a lot of discussion boards out there, on every subject imaginable (and I mean every subject). All you have to do is contact the moderator or the webmaster, ask them permission, and then go through it with the search feature -- and before long, you could have a book. For example: I could go to wine spectator sites and ask them if I could do that. They have all these questions and answers about wine already available. So I could whip out a booklet about how to find a good bottle of wine for under $10, then give them a copy, and I'd have a copy, and we could both sell it.

Here's another option: go to a seminar and offer to speak for free if you can have the rights -- or shared rights -- to your video and to the other speakers' videos. Most of these seminars provide a free video of all the talks, so they can sell them. I've spoken at quite a few of them myself. **In one weekend you can walk away with half a dozen to a dozen video products from all kinds of experts.** You spend a few days at the seminar, you listen to all the other speakers' ideas, then you go home and it's done.

Once Isn't Enough!

One thing I want you to keep in mind, however you create your product, is that product is power; do whatever you can to build up your product base. **The number of products you have equals the potential income in your pocket, so I want to offer a wealth-building shortcut that I think is the real lazy person's secret for creating informational products.** Here's what it is: you recycle your old information. That's how easy it is. I hit on this a little bit before, but I want to elaborate on it here.

First of all, a basic truism in our field: it's easier to recycle old material than it is to create something new from scratch. You can create a whole bunch of different informational products by using bits and pieces of your old products. You can write or record something once, and get paid for it dozens and dozens of times. If you think about it, this gives you the same kind of leverage that many of the world's richest people have. **They do something one time, and then they get paid for it over and over**. For example, famous authors will write a book and get paid for many years for that book. Movie stars, movie producers, or other types of investors also do something one time, and are able to earn a stream of income from it for many years. The information publishing business lets you do this, too.

You can get paid many times for each page that you write, or for every recording you produce. The customers don't care -- I know this for a fact. Whenever we start talking about recycling old informational products, some people say, "Hey, you're ripping your customers off, because you're charging them twice for something you did once!" Well, many customers don't buy every single product that you produce, first of all; and second, if you're just taking a few pages out of one book and putting it in another, they're not likely to notice. **But what they are going to notice is value, and that's all they really want.** They're going to notice that you put a lot of value into your product; they're not going to notice that you took pages 90-100 out of one book and put it in another. Of course, if anyone complains, you can do something to make it right. But we've been doing this for years, and we're doing more and more of it all the time -- and we've yet to receive any complaints whatsoever for recycling information.

All you really have to do here is find as many ways as

you can to recycle your old material. A chapter from one book could be a chapter in another book. Excerpts from one recording can be used in other recordings. The printed transcripts from one recording could be used in any manual that you do. Small reports can be added together to create new material. Single audiotapes can easily be grouped together, just by having an editor take out excerpts and doing some re-recording in between those sound bites.

Here's a quick example of how M.O.R.E., Inc. has done this. A few years back, we committed to producing fifty-one new informational products in five months. Somebody who doesn't understand these shortcut techniques might say, "My God, how in the world were you able to produce that many informational products in five months?" Well, one of the ways we did it was by recycling that old information. **We transcribed some audio tapes, mixed some new material in there, and in a fraction of the time it would take to produce a product from scratch, we were able to have brand-new products.** Also, because we've built our products up over the years, we had about fifteen hundred pages of material that we could go back to and take a few pages from here, a few pages there, and we re-mix it into a new form.

When you create new integrated products, they offer great value to the customer, even if they include some elements of older products. Not only does the customer not feel cheated, but the customer is ecstatic! **They're extremely happy, because we've taken the bits and the pieces from the best of other materials and joined them together to create new materials.** For example, we've got several hundred audio tapes we've produced over the years, and we're finding all kinds of ways to use the printed transcripts to create new manuals, and also to create new audio recordings out of the sound bites of the old audio tapes. That's our secret. It's a real lazy man's approach. Just remember: it's always easier to recycle something than to come up with something from scratch. Of course, you may not have the backlog of products that we do. **That's when I think you need to go out and get other people to share their products with you.** You can produce them, tape them, and make CDs, or take cassette tapes and turn them into manuals. If you already have product, you're already set to continually create more streams of income from the products you have, just by repackaging them.

Authors have been doing this for years and years: the most successful authors and publishers continually bring out reissues of older volumes or combine the best of their existing work. Musicians also do it to: look at the "best of" albums that are released by every major recording artist. They put out five albums, and then they release a "best of" album. All that involves is pulling songs off of the previous releases and creating a new product.

Here's an excellent example from my friend and colleague Alan Bechtold. More than 30 years ago, he was involved in a limited edition chapbook series featuring famous science fiction authors, where each did an original story for each little book. **Alan didn't have much money then, but he did have a lot of determination.** He actually wrote to Isaac Asimov, the famous science fiction author, and offered him $200 if he'd write Alan an original story and agree to sign 500 of those little hardbound books. Asimov amazed Alan by agreeing -- and this was one of the biggest names in science fiction. He said, "Hey, you just caught me off -guard. I really like the idea, so I'll write the story." Alan tells me he kind of apologized later when he sent him the $200, saying, "I know it's not a lot of money," but Asimov replied, "I'm not worried about that. First thing I'm going to do is resell it to Isaac Asimov's Science Fiction Magazine, and I'm going to use it in at least four other books." The point is,

Asimov had his marketing all figured out for that story far down the road; he just thought that Alan's idea was a neat way to launch it.

In a similar way, when my colleague Don Bice created his first product, someone asked him, "Will each chapter stand alone as a separate product?" Don said, "What? I never even considered that." The other guy replied, "Yeah, look at it this way. **Write your book, but make sure you get at least eight or nine separate products out of that, even just printed products.** If you take chapters out of that publication and re-title them, will they stand alone? If they can't, then go back and look at what you plan to do, because you should get another bunch of products out of that." That was his first exposure to this idea; until then, he says, it never crossed his mind. But it's a tremendous concept, because if you do ten chapters and they stand alone, in addition to getting ten products in addition to the book, you also can take those ten chapters and turn them into ten articles in magazines. Just tell the magazine publishers that at the end of the article, you want a resource box that tells people that this is a chapter from your book and if they send $29.95, you'll send them the complete book.

I recall reading about one magazine -- I believe it was Family Circle -- whose most popular column over all the years was, "Can This Marriage Be Saved?" Women love to read that kind of column, because they can learn every month about how other women have overcome their marital troubles. So, what if you went to that magazine and said, "Hey, let's put all those articles into a book and call it "Can This Marriage Be Saved?" Have twenty-four or thirty-six of them, and sell them in one package. **Because, you see, what people are most interested in, by and large, is other people.** With the advent of the Internet, it becomes amazingly easy to reach people and to communicate with them, and to have them just simply write stuff for you and then email it to your website. **You let other people share their experiences, their strengths, their ideas.** If you want to do a book with ten chapters, you can get ten consultants together, and have them each write an article.

Invite Content from Your Readers

From a marketing perspective, the best thing about the Internet is that it makes these shortcut systems even shorter. Certainly, you could use all these ideas before the Internet; but by using the Internet, you're cutting down on your product creation time even more. You can email a lot of these authors instantly, and get a response back quickly. You can do some research and find existing articles online. **Sure, you could take some of these shortcut ideas with no computer at all and create a product within two weeks or a month; but with access to the Internet, you can have it ready even more quickly.** Now you're creating a product in a couple days. I think tying these shortcut ideas in with the Internet is the perfect marriage.

And, you know, the topic can be anything! There's a guy in El Paso, Texas who puts out books, videos and audio recordings about alien visitation. When I saw the catalog of his offers, I noticed that many were based on stuff submitted by readers: close encounters of the third kind. **All he does is ask his readers to submit their stories regarding alien visitation.** I didn't know that belief in alien visitation was that common, but plenty of people say they've been visited or even kidnapped by these little guys. Maybe some of them make up the stories; maybe some of them believe they're true. Who knows? In any case, he was creating all kinds of books and booklets just from what his readers submitted. So you see, it doesn't

---

have to be moneymaking, cookbooks, home business -- it can be any one of a thousand and one topics.

Here's another example: www.joke-of-the-day.com. This is a site that's been around for years. **Every time the guy who runs it sends out a joke by email, he makes money, because he sells advertising that goes along with the joke.** He has hundreds of thousands of people around the world who read his jokes, and they send him more. Take a look, and you'll see that every single one is tagged something like this: "This joke was submitted by Joe Blow in Cincinnati." They send him the joke, and he sends it to hundreds of thousands of others, along with an advertisement for software or whatever. He's making a fortune, and he doesn't have to come up with any of the material! What a fun job! **One of our friends in the business calls this the Tom Sawyer principle, because in the book "Tom Sawyer," if you recall, Tom got his buddies to paint the fence for him while he sat back and relaxed -- and got paid for it.** People like that kind of thing so much. Here's a good example: the guys who made millions with Chicken Soup for the Soul. All they're doing is tapping into this huge desire that most people have for recognition, attention, wanting to be heard, wanting to be published, wanting to see their names in print. They fall over themselves to share their stories. When you watch a ball game on TV and the camera pans the crowd, they go crazy. They just want to be seen for one second; forget about the fifteen minutes of fame Andy Warhol mentioned. **They want one second. Well, when someone writes an article, or a report, or submits material for a book and gets to see their name and story in print -- man, they get excited.**

The thing that I think is interesting about this is you can make it work with any hobby. Let's take golf, for example; just go get some free publicity and collect hundreds of peoples' favorite golf stories, and you can

---

publish a book about that. It works if you like arts and crafts, flea markets, fishing, knitting -- there are tons of options from which to chose. **Anybody who has any kind of hobby could find stories from people in that particular hobby market, and create a book for which they don't have to do any writing for.**

Don Bice has a friend who's a magician, and he publishes magic books. Now, this is hobby area about which people are passionate. **When you find a hobby area like that, you'll find people who want to be in print and who want people to know that their articles come from an expert.** So Don's friend collects stories and articles from other magicians, and has published maybe 45 or 50 titles over the last few years, with the books selling anywhere from $10 to $100. Not in a single case has a contributor asked for a dime -- not even with the books that sell for over $100. Don's friend does a very high quality job, makes them very attractive, and gives the authors a nice quantity of books -- generally about a dozen. They're so thrilled to see the beautiful job in print, and he ends up with more manuscripts than he can handle.

So unleash your creativity, folks; learn to recycle your own old information, and especially, let other people do the work for you! You can get projects completed amazingly quick this way, rapidly allowing for multiple streams of income from many different products on which you didn't even do any of the actual work. The people who buy those products perceive that they're getting tremendous value. <u>That's the real secret to producing viable products by using these shortcuts; you have to give people tremendous value</u>.

Chapter Four

Freedom, Glorious Freedom!

In this chapter, I want to start off by directing you to another great source of information that's yours for the picking, almost always free, and can be used in any way that you want. This is the Consumer Information Center out of Pueblo, Colorado. You've seen all the ads, the little consumer information booklets, pamphlets, and what have you that you can order for fifty cents or a buck. They've got millions. The Consumer Information Center is basically just an outlet for the federal government's publication service; you can find their website at http://www.pueblo.gsa.gov. It's divided into simple, easily-searched categories: Cars, Children, Education, Employment, Housing, Health, Food, Money, Small Business, Travel, And More (yes, there's a button called "And More..."). There are dozens of pamphlets in each category that you can order online.

But you don't really have to order a thing. What's wonderful about web technology is that you can read these pamphlets right online, or even download them in an Adobe Acrobat format -- which means they're already typeset and looking really good. Now, here's the big secret. **When the federal government produces one of these booklets, it cannot copyright that material.** <u>**Since it was produced with taxpayer dollars, that material's owned by every citizen of the United States -- including you**</u>.

I want to caution you: some of the information made available by the Consumer Information Center in Pueblo are actually produced and copyrighted by various companies for the federal government. They may place a restriction on a particular piece of information, saying it's free to use only for educational purposes; most, however, are yours free of charge. **Admittedly, there's one drawback to this information: most of it's deadly dry and boring.** It's filled with the kind of facts, figures, and information you need from federal government agencies, but it's not entertaining. **The good news is, you can wrap that info into your own products very easily, and flesh out and use snippets of it, or reference it if needed.** One of the things I find fascinating is that some of these pamphlets are actually designed as very pretty websites that stand on their own. **You can put together links on your website that jump to these pages and offer the information as if it was from your website.** You wouldn't even have to take the information -- just push people over to it.

The reason I say this info is dry is due to what it's missing. **Remember, the one thing people most want to know about is other people.** They want information, sure, but the real power of having other people create your product for you is that it's real people doing it. You've got a number of people involved in that product, people telling war stories about how they've survived this or that or come up with this or that new technique or new idea. **The information is being imparted through real people who've experienced it, and that's what people want to hear.** Look at <u>People Magazine</u>. When I first saw an issue, I thought, Man, what an idiot idea. That shows what I know! Nowadays <u>People</u> is one of the most popular magazines in America. The bottom line is that everybody wants to know all about people.

Another thing you should attempt to do -- and I've touched on this before -- is to set up a win-win situation with your publishing venture. Earlier I mentioned putting together a contest, and working with companies to provide the prizes for you. In return, you mention in all of your promotion materials that they're putting up the prizes. You give them a page in the book, or you give away books to them, or a special prize to the people that contribute to your book. Then there's the great idea (which I stole from Don Bice!) of directing people to a website to get a checklist. **Again, you're setting up, whenever you can, a win-win situation where you benefit, and the person providing you with what you're drawing from also benefits.** It always works like magic.

Even using the government material, it's still a win-win situation. **Don't look at it as if you're stealing material; you're helping the government accomplish their goal of circulating their material.** The government wants to get it in the hands of as many people as will benefit; that's their purpose in publishing it, and really, they don't do a very good job of distribution. **Many a mail order company has done more to promote circulation of government publications than the government ever has on their own.** So if you can use any of those government publications -- and there are some great ones -- don't have any reservations about doing so, because you're promoting their goals of getting it into the hands of as many people as possible in the first place.

The Writing Process

Next, I'd like to discuss the actual writing process, something I offered a few tips on back in Chapter 2. **No matter what type of information product you create, at some point you're going to have to do a little writing -- whether it's an introduction, a summary, a cover, or an article of your own.** As I pointed out previously, for many people that's a point of tremendous fear; but the truth is, the hard part about writing is just getting started. Sitting down with paper and pen -- or at that blank computer screen -- and getting the first words down can be sheer torture. It doesn't matter whether you're an experienced writer or beginner, you'll still have the same fear.

The most prolific writer in modern history was Walter B. Gibson. Walter wrote all the "Shadow" novels, as well as a lot of how-to information. His house literally had rooms with bookcases from floor to ceiling that were stacked with books that Walter had written. He was always writing books. **He had trouble getting started, so the way he got started writing was that he never stopped -- he just kept going from page to page to page.** He had typewriters throughout his house, and would have several books going at any one time. He'd walk by one typewriter and work there for a half hour or so, then he'd move to another typewriter and work on a different book. Someone once asked him, "Walter, why don't you just sit in front of one typewriter, and take the pages out and change them when you switch from one book to the next?" He would say, "And waste all that time? No way." So he got up and moved from typewriter to typewriter instead.

Most of us aren't going to write that way, but like the rest of us, Walter didn't like to get started, and this was his way of making an end run around that problem. So, how do you get started? **Well, first, the most important thing is to make an agreement with yourself that you're not going to write a perfect page, you're not going to write a perfect opening, and nobody will ever see what you put on this first piece of paper except you.** You're not going to correct it, it's not going to get graded, it's not going to get printed; just sit down and say to yourself, "I'm going to write the introduction, first paragraph, or the first page to this introduction or manual," or whatever it is you need to write. Sit down and play with that first paragraph or page. Don't check the grammar, don't check the spelling, and don't polish it. It's much easier to write when you give yourself permission to do it that way. Then, when you do finish that first page and take time to read it, study it very carefully -- but don't look at the grammar, don't look at the spelling, and don't judge it. Look for the good idea, or the nice thought, or the clever introduction, or look for something else buried in the contents that you like. **When you see something in it that you like, congratulate yourself, say, "Hey, that's pretty good" -- and then wad up the paper and throw it away. Now start over.**

I know that doesn't sound like a shortcut, but believe me, it is! What you've done is gotten over the hurdle; you've gotten started, you've blown out all the crud that was in the pipes, and you've done just like an athlete preparing for contest. You stretched your muscles, you're warmed up, and you're ready to write.

You might think that the next thing to do is to write the second paragraph or the second page, but that's not true. **Write the conclusion to your publication.** Sit down and write exactly how this publication is going to end: the last paragraph, or the last two or three paragraphs, whatever is comfortable for you. Take as much time as you need. Again, don't judge; and when you finish, polish and make it as good as you possibly can. Now you have a beginning, and you have an end. You've got a start that you're happy with, and you've got a conclusion that you're proud of. At this point, something goes to work that I can't explain. **Your mind makes that whole writing process easier, because it knows where it's going and how it's going to wind up.** There's something about our minds that will give us the information we need to just connect the dots in the middle.

You've got an outline, or a plan, or notes; it'll just flow into place. I know it sounds silly, but the truth is that this can lessen the pain of writing and improve your writing at the same time.

A couple of other tips: first, don't correct your writing as you proceed. Let's say you're writing a chapter or a section; don't evaluate as you go. Most of us type a word and we see it's incorrect and we change it, or we say, "No, no, I need to change my grammar here." Don't do that! Concentrate on content, not on the form, and write as rapidly as you can. Make an agreement with yourself that you won't make any corrections until you finish. There's a really sound psychological reason for doing that. A person's mind is basically divided into two hemispheres, one that controls the creative processes and another that controls our analytical processes. They overlap somewhat, but generally it's the right side controls the creative process, and that's the part that's doing the writing. The left side is the judgment side.

Well, if you're writing and you're absorbed in your thoughts about the content and you suddenly say, "Oh, that word is wrong," you've switched hemispheres. You're now thinking critically. The critical side of you is the side that's already telling you that you can't write, that this is hard. The creative side may be enjoying the process, and the critical side ruins that. **So make an agreement with yourself and promise you'll honor it: you won't do any self-criticisms, evaluations, reread, or change grammar until you've finished the section you're working on.** Do this, and you'll find that your writing will flow much faster, much easier, and will become fun.

Here's another little point about the writing process. When you're new to it, it's a good idea to try to write after some model, some author whose style and technical skill you admire. While you're not plagiarizing -- that's a definite no-no -- you don't have to start with a blank page. Otherwise, if you're not sure how to get started, or how to organize things, or there are a lot of different questions on your mind, do some research. **There's a lot of information about getting started out there, written by famous authors who are making millions of dollars.** They tell you exactly how they do it. You can go through their different processes, figure out what's best for you, then start using those processes yourself in your own writing.

Recycling Redux

This next idea harks back to what I said in the last chapter about using information again and again -- but it takes it in a slightly different direction. **One of the things you can do with existing information that you've created or otherwise own is to take a product and change the niche -- that is, change the product in such a way that you can sell it to an entirely new group of people.** When you do this, you're not doing a whole lot of new writing with your product; maybe you're writing a new introduction or summary, and that's it. But you're selling it to an entirely new group of people, people who've never seen that product before.

For example, let's say you've written a book about discount travel, how to save money on vacations. Let's say that you're selling this book specifically to seniors; there's a large senior market out there, so you've written or compiled a book called "The Senior's Guide to Discount Travel," and you're selling tons of them. Suppose your sales are slacking off a bit. Look around and see who else might profit from discount travel of the kind you're selling; for example, business travelers. That's another good market. You may have to change the introduction a little, but you can leave 95% of it intact -- because after all, it's all about getting discount travel. **Now you can re-title it and sell it in business magazines.** Later, maybe you can change the introduction again and call it "The Adventurer's Guide to Discount Travel" and advertise it in cycling or skydiving magazines. **Again, you retain the same 95% of the information, maybe changing the introduction and a few words around, and sell it to a different niche market instead of the niche to which you're already selling it.**

Here's a real-life example of a marketing company that's been doing a great job of this and making it very simple. They had quite a bit of information on mail order marketing, and then the Internet popped up and became huge, and tons of people wanted to know how to do Internet marketing. Well, what they did was take all their mail order marketing information and deleted all the references to mail order, popping in the word "Internet" in its place. Immediately they had an Internet marketing course that sold incredibly well to people interested in that field. It was a very good course, too, because the reality is that marketing for both the Internet and mail order (and other types of areas as well) are very similar. Instead of having to write an entirely brand new course on Internet marketing, they were able to make very simple changes to an existing course and immediately have a new course that they could sell.

There's also a company that created books on How to Get Freebies. **They did exactly the same thing: instead of just creating a new book on freebies every time, they retained 95% of the information on how to get free things, and then they titled each book differently so they could sell it to a different niche.** They have "The Senior's Guide to Freebies," "The Teacher's Guide to Freebies," "The Kid's Guide to Freebies," and "The Parent's Guide to

Freebies," all of which contain basically the same information but target different niches. **Once again, by taking a basic block of information and changing maybe just the introduction and a few things inside the package, you can actually sell it to different niches and make a lot of money with basically the same product.** I really want to hammer that home, because I feel it's such a good idea, a powerful idea that saves you time and energy but can bring in a lot of extra profit.

Good Help is So Easy to Find

Let's go back and take another look at the idea of getting other people to do all the work for you. I talked earlier about various projects that lend themselves to that strategy: home business, cookbooks, even alien visitations. **Probably the best way to get the ball rolling is to start with a news release that you send to various publications, or an announcement that you post on various Internet websites and newsgroups.** Of course, you have to send it to those sites or those specialty publications most likely to have the kind of people that would respond and help you write your books and other information products you want to produce; a shotgun approach isn't going to help here.

In the world of travel, you could send out releases announcing that you want information from people on how to travel free, or almost free. **Once you get enough great ideas, you publish them and then send a copy to everyone that submitted materials.** You could also easily do something on the best place on earth to go on vacation; that's something a lot of people would want to learn. Then you can get into hunting and fishing: "My Greatest Hunting Experience," "My Greatest Fishing Experience," "How I Caught the Most Bass," or "My

Greatest Sea Fishing Experience."

Or how about something like "Secrets To A Happy Marriage," where you ask people who have been married 40 years or more and still haven't killed each other how they did it? Plenty of older couples would submit material that you could publish as part of a great informational product. Where would you go to find them? Place a call for submissions in the senior publications and any senior websites you find. If you want to publish on hobbies and unusual moneymaking hobbies, then track down the appropriate publications and any hobby sites on the Internet and ask for submissions. How about a publication called "The Very Best Place to Meet Single Women?" How many millions of guys would buy that book or that manual? Well, go to the men's publications for information. The reverse, of course, is "The Very Best Places to Meet Single Men," and for that you go to the women's publications or any women's sites. You can go right down the list. Let's say you wanted to get into the Christian market, which is huge. Well, you could ask for submissions on the topic "Why I Know There's a God." You'd be surprised, I think, the number of submissions you'd receive from the readers of Christian websites and Christian publications. Or how about, "Returning from Eternity," where you go to metaphysical sites and publications and ask people for their near-death experiences? I think there's a vast marketplace for that, because I know that books on the subject have sold millions of copies.

Here's a similar idea. To find people with the stories you need, run an ad saying something like, "Have you had a successful weight loss? Have you gone on a diet and taken off X amount of pounds and kept it off for over a year? If so, we want you to be included in this new book." **You could interview the top ten, or fifty, or hundred people and put together a collection like I talked about earlier, focusing**

on successful, proven-in-the-real-world diets that worked for people to lose weight. I think that would be bestseller.

Something similar is produced regularly by <u>Guidepost</u> magazine, which publishes something called "Angels on Earth." There's such a big interest in angels that people send in their stories and talk about how they believe that their guardian angels saved them from a car accident, or helped them find their long lost brother, or what have you. The magazine collects and publishes these stories, along with profiles and stories about people who do things that would make you say, "What an Angel, to do such a nice thing for other people!" <u>Their whole publication is written by their readers</u>.

The Shortest of Shortcuts

Did you know that about fifty thousand books are published each year? It's true. Only a few hundred are actually big enough sellers to be financially successful, but that doesn't mean all the other thousands are losers. **So here's an idea: find one of these poor-selling but great books, then go to the publisher and get permission to promote it by mail or on the Internet.** I think that's a tremendous opportunity for someone to mine a vein that the publisher originally missed. A good, vigorous online campaign can turn books like this into best-selling products when they're marketed to the right niche.

The way you can do this is to go to the bookstore and look for books that are sitting on the 75% off sale table. Maybe they've been out a few months, maybe even just a few weeks, and they just aren't selling well enough, so the publisher says, "Mark them down and get them out of there."

Find a book on a topic that's interesting to you, or that you know there's really a huge niche market for -- one in which a lot of people are interested in. **Go ahead and buy it, then write to the publisher and make a deal with them. You'll probably be pleasantly surprised.** You see, most publishers focus on the one or two books a year that are the big winners by the big fiction authors, and don't really bother to promote everything else very hard. Just go to them and tell them you're not interested in selling it in the bookstores; you just want the rights to sell it by mail and on the Internet. Maybe they'll charge you a few hundred or a few thousand dollars, but that can be an excellent investment; because if you have the right title, you can go ahead and sell thousands of copies of it.

Here's a great example of just that from Mark Nolan, using one of the greatest marketing tools ever invented: the press release. **Mark wrote a book called "Instant Cash Flow," which basically boils down to, "find a product, write a press release, send it out, get publicity."** One guy who ordered his book, Lee Michaels, called Mark up and he said, "I don't have a product." That led to Mark's instant information product idea; what he told Lee was, "Well, if you want to sell a book, do you know where all the books are?" Lee said, "Where?" and Mark replied, "They're in the bookstore." After Lee stopped laughing, Mark told him, "I'm serious."

So Lee went to the bookstore. He was interested in working at home; Mark told him that most of those work at home things are just a joke, but he did find a book called "The Work At Home Source Book" by Lynnie Arden. It had been written up in <u>Parenting Magazine</u>, and it was in the book clubs and had gotten good reviews, because it was one of the few real books that could list companies that would allow people to work at home. He decided that was the book he'd try to sell, since it hadn't done all that well in the initial go-round, even though it was well-received. So he wrote a news release, bought a roll of stamps, and he mailed it out. He ended up getting the book written up in magazines and newspapers all over.

Notably, he was written up in Working Mother. Initially, he hadn't intended to send it there, but Mark told him he should. He said, "Gee, the book was already written up in Parenting, so why would I send it to Working Mother?" Mark said, "Well, that proves it's good for parents, but somehow they missed that magazine." (When Mark talked to the author later, she said, "We sent one to each, but Working Mother just didn't run it.") This just goes to show that it's important to try, try again. Lee wrote his release to mirror closely the story that was in Parenting, and this time Working Mother picked it up. The result was that he pulled in $27,000 for this book.

He just bought them from the wholesaler, like all the bookstores do; so the book was already written, it was already in print, it was already available wholesale. He didn't have to buy the rights to it, because it was already there for anybody who wanted to buy it wholesale. All Lee did was write to the publisher and say, "I'm in the mail order business. Please send me your discount rate schedule and vendor application." They sent him a sheet saying, "When you buy 1 to 10 copies it costs this much, when you buy 50 you'll get this discount, when you buy 100 you'll get this discount." He didn't buy any; he just had a couple on hand that he had purchased at the store. Then, when the orders poured in, he called them up and asked them to send him a few hundred by UPS 3-Day Select. **Three days later he had inventory, paid for by his customers in advance -- so he's out no money except for the roll of stamps, and he's made a tidy profit!**

So that people didn't think that he'd gotten struck by lightning, he decided to do it again. This time he found another book called "Dollars at Home Directory." It comes with a video, too. He sent out news releases, and one release was picked up by a syndicated columnist -- a column like that goes into many newspapers, it's not just one. This one column alone brought in $34,690. From one news release! **So he turned a postage stamp, one postage stamp that you can borrow from your neighbor, into $34,000 and change with a product that was already written and available in bookstores.** So why don't people just go down to the bookstore and buy it? Because they're lazy, and they see that it's so easy to order through the mail. Besides, they don't think, "Maybe I should go down to the bookstore and get this."

That's the shortest of shortcuts: to find a product that's already in existence, like a book, and to write or call the publisher or manufacturer and see about buying some in bulk, for a discount, and selling them yourself. By the end of the day, you could have a product, write a news release, and you could be mailing it. That's fast and instant and immediate, and there's no risk or cost except for some stamps. The effort involved is just what it takes to type up eight lines of type into a news release. That's what Mark Nolan tells everybody to do in his book, and that's why his book sold 100,000 copies. **If you can go to the bookstore and find a book you like -- any book on any subject in the non-fiction section -- you can be selling it through free publicity in just a few days.**

Chapter Five

Take Action!

The last story in Chapter Four is a great lead-in to the point I want to emphasize in this chapter: in order to make anything happen in business, using shortcuts or not, you have to get moving and take action. **The one thing besides a couple of books and a big roll of stamps that Lee Michaels had was initiative.** When you study the lives of all the people who've made it big in just about anything, you'll find that these are people who've made a habit of taking action -- sometime audacious, bold action. A lot of people have great ideas in the shower, but by the time they dry off and get dressed, the idea is gone. A lot of people have great ideas, but how many people take action?

In this final chapter, I want to urge you to look back at all the techniques I've revealed here, study them, and take them very seriously. Then put them into action. Your plan doesn't have to be perfect from the git-go; it just has to be good enough to get started. **And the fact is, you don't have to go all-out right from the beginning; one of the best things about marketing is that you can ease into it, and build your business as you learn.** <u>But you do have to start</u>. Try to use some of the techniques that I've discussed here to develop product every single day.

Here's the basic principle: all you do is invest a small amount of time into developing new products every day. It's really simple; just put it into your schedule. Do it at the same time every day, like when you first get up in the morning and you're drinking coffee. Listen to this: if you just write one page every day, that's over 300 pages a year! How long is it going to take you to write one page? Well, that depends. It may be slow going at first, but you do build up steam. Some people can write a page in 10 minutes, some people 45 minutes. On average, let's say it takes 30 to 45 minutes a day to get a nice page written. That's not bad, because in a year you've got 300 pages added to your product arsenal! Or, if you're like we are and you like to do audio recordings -- which is an easy way to record information -- you can spend 15 minutes a day recording. It may take you 20 minutes to come up with the notes that you're going to work from to do your 15 minutes of recording, but you do that for five days a week. Spend 30 minutes in front of a microphone five days a week, and every month you're going to produce eight 45-minute audio recordings. <u>Like Nike likes to say, you just do it.</u> **You put it into your schedule, and soon you're developing products that you know your customers will want to buy.** If you create eight audio recordings, that's equivalent to 150-175 transcribed pages of new material that you can have edited and printed, plus the eight recordings. And, if you use the concept that I shared with you earlier, you can recycle all of that information and use it again and again. **So think of this almost as a hobby, but do it every single day. You'll get good at it, and it starts becoming fun.**

My father's wife took one look at one of the first products we ever produced, threw it on the floor, and said, "This is crap." It really embarrassed me, my Dad, and Eileen -- but the fact was, she was right. I can look back on it years later and say she was right, because it was just a little thing, inexpensively printed, full of typos. **But to the customers who bought it, it was really good, helpful information.** We did upgrade that product, and it went through seven or eight editions, and finally it ended up being a great product in the end. But let me re-emphasize that it doesn't have to be good, it just has to be good enough. So give yourself a break here. What you're selling is information. Nobody expects you to be a great writer or a great communicator. What they expect you to do is give value for the money, and it helps, of course, if you really have an interest in what you're writing or communicating about, because your customers can sense that. I think that's one of the most important things, in fact; your enthusiasm will make up for any liabilities.

One of my heroes, Dan Kennedy, is a guy who produces many, many different informational products. He's got about ten books in the bookstores, and he's always coming up with new things. About 15 years ago Eileen and I sat down with him at a Mexican restaurant in Phoenix, Arizona, and I asked him, "Dan, how in the world do you come up with all this material?" He said, "I get up every day at 5:00 in the morning, and by 5:05 a.m. every morning I'm writing. Every day I do that for 45 minutes. I don't care whether I'm feeling great, or I'm feeling sick, or I stayed up until 3:00 in the morning the day before and I'm dead tired. I just do it every single day, and it builds up." That's a simple concept, and if nothing else, I hope that's something that you, as a reader, take away from this book when you're done reading it. **A little bit at a time can really add up, no matter which of the techniques that I've discussed here you decide to use.** If you just use them a little bit every day, you're going to build something that's going to be worth a tremendous amount of money.

One of the things that struck me as I put together this publication was how easily the ideas flowed. It's easy enough now to come up with dozens of ideas that have a chance to make a good amount of money. Back before I started in this business, more than twenty years ago, it wasn't that way for me at all. **I could never think of anything to sell.** It wasn't so much that I didn't want to do the work, I was just agonizing over, "What can I sell? What can I sell?" Most of the people I talk to these days have the same problem: they're asking, "What can I create? What can I come up with?" My impression is that they've never taken the time to sit down and develop an idea. What they really mean is that nothing has interrupted their consciousness long enough to say, "This is what you should do. This is what you should write." **They equate getting an idea with inspiration -- the light bulb above the head that we see in cartoons.** The light goes on and they say, "Aha, that's it!"

The truth is that for me -- and I'm sure this is true for other professional marketers -- the ideas come because I sit down and say, "OK, I have to work at an idea." **So I devote some time to thinking about the issue, and some ideas inevitably come up.** Admittedly, some are better than others; some really stink. But if you do that frequently, you'll have more products to create, and it gets easier with time. I'm living proof. When I started out, I spent all my time worrying that I needed a product. Now that I've developed this mental approach of spending some time every day thinking about it, my problem is just the opposite -- I find that there are more ideas for products than I can pursue in a lifetime. My problem now is how to pick the best ones.

It can happen to you, too; I don't believe I'm anything special in this regard. So sit down every morning, drink some coffee, and start filling up a notebook with ideas. If you have a book full of ideas, it's going to make it so much easier to get started with actual product creation. One thing I want to point out here is that, no matter how difficult writing seems to most of the people on the outside, it's common knowledge among most writers that the actual act of writing is, itself, quite easy. **You just have to write; you have to start. That's the hard part!** Half the people in the world who want to write for a living, or produce products, never get past that obstacle. So the moment you start, when you've got those first pages rolling, you just beat 50% of the people out there who wish they could. Once you're past that, just write every day. It's one of those things I've always done. **You write every day, even if it's just half a page or whatever you can make the time for.** You'll find that even 20 minutes a day can turn into a book in a year.

Next -- and this is extremely important -- you have to finish what you write. **Half the people who actually get over that first hurdle and get started never finish what they write.** So if you can finish a work, you're head and shoulders above 75-90% of the people who wish they could write in the first place. The beauty of the shortcut ideas I've given you in this book is that if you're writing that page or two every day, and all you have to come up with is the introduction and tie all the different pieces together, then you can turn 20 minutes a day turn into five books a year. The daily chore is really the secret.

Back in Chapter 3, I mentioned a friend of Don Bice, a man who writes and sells tricks to professional magicians. Most of the big illusions you see on television specials, like the vanishing Statue of Liberty, are his ideas. **He's made a very good income from selling those ideas. He just sits down every day for an hour, opens a composition book, and brainstorms ideas and writes things down as they occur to him.** Most of them aren't really developed ideas. Most of them aren't even good ideas, but he does this every day. Then when there's a need for something, when somebody comes to him and says, "I really need an idea for this," and describes what they're looking for, he simply goes back to his composition books and reviews those ideas and evaluates them as he goes. He goes back and finds the right pieces, and then he has an idea that he refines and gives to them. The secret is that his mind is trained to think of new stuff every day. He doesn't worry whether it's good or not at the time; he evaluates it when it comes time to use it. You can do the same thing with product ideas. **Just jot down some ideas every day. In the beginning, it's probably going to be very difficult; at least, it was for me.** Over time, you exercise that creative muscle; and as long as it's not a matter of life and death, where you're forced to come up with an idea immediately, the ideas just flow. As the great Joe Crossman likes to say, "Everything's difficult until it becomes easy."

The hardest thing in this regard is to look at a blank page -- but when you write one sentence on that page, you're about half done with the job! Earlier, I spoke about Alan Bechtold's experiences with Isaac Asimov, which really impressed me. Asimov passed away a few years back, but until his death he was one of the most prolific writers in the history of authorship. He wrote hundreds and hundreds of books; in fact, he was credited in the Guinness Book of World Records as writing a 500-page book in three days. **Someone asked him once, "I'd love to be a writer. What's the best advice you can give me?"** <u>Asimov replied, "Write! If you're going to be a writer, write."</u>

I think I've provided you with a lot of good suggestions here, what I believe are great tips and strategies to get other people to do most of creative work for you. **But you're going to have to do at least some of the work yourself, so you're going to have to write.** The best way to do it is to just start. You're not creating the Great American Novel. You're not writing "Gone with the Wind." You're putting simple information on paper, you're writing the way you speak, and that's all it takes to get the job done and to make a lot of money. **Self publishers are making more money than almost anyone these days!** There are 300 or 400 self-published authors that are millionaires, and their books sell well. There are a few thousand other authors, mostly of how-to books, who are making good money. Self-publishing is a great, great way to go.

And I think that's a great place to end this publication. I hope you've enjoyed reading it, and I want to urge you to go read it again and again. Take notes every time you go through it. **Remember, these techniques have made me literally millions of dollars; and the same is true for the other half-dozen members of the panel discussion this publication is based on.** I think they can make you millions of dollars, too. The secret is to get started, to put these ideas into action, and to always continue to find new ideas and new ways of doing things!

www.ingramcontent.com/pod-product-compliance
Lightning Source LLC
Chambersburg PA
CBHW032016190326
41520CB00007B/492